Options Trading Basics

For the everyday investors

Dr. Adan Abbasi

"Options Trading Made Simple" breaks down the barriers to entry into the world of options trading, offering a unique, hands-on guide for everyday investors. Recognizing a gap in the market for an accessible entry point, this workbook simplifies the trading process, removing the intimidation factor and making it easy to learn and trade. Through practical exercises and clear explanations, it empowers readers to confidently navigate the market, manage risks, and capitalize on opportunities to enhance their financial standing. It's more than a learning tool; it's your roadmap to trading success.

WHAT ARE OPTIONS

Options are **contracts** on the shares of a company on the stock market.

Options are also called "**Derivatives**" because their price is derived from the price of the stock.

Where & How to Trade Options

Options are traded on the stock markets like NASDAQ, NYSE, and CBOE.

You can trade Options using iPhone Apps:

RobinHood App

weBull App

TastyTrades App

Why trade Options

Options give potential for much higher profits but also come with higher risks.

Options can also be used to generate cash income in the stock market.

Options are also used as a means of protection against drops in stock prices.

MAIN USES OF OPTIONS

Speculation

Income Generation

Protection (Hedging)

BULLS VS BEARS

Bull market: Market or a stock price is likely to go up.

Bear Market: Market or a stock price is likely to go Down.

TYPES OF OPTIONS

There are 2 types of options:

"Call" Options

"Put" Options

"Call" Options make money if stock price of the company goes up.

"Put" Options make money if stock price of the company goes down.

This is also referred to as the **option type**.

Pop Quiz # 1

If the market is bullish about a company stock (i.e. stock price is expected to go up)

Do you buy a "Call" or "Put" Option?

The correct answer is "Call" Option since its price goes up when the stock price of the company goes up. You can lose all your investment if the market does not move up soon enough.

Expiration Date

All Options have an Expiration Date.

Options usually expire 30, 60, 90 days or 1, 2 years. These options usually expire on the 3rd Friday of each month.

Some Options expire the same day and are called 0-DTE options. (0 Days-To-Expiration)

Expiration Time

On the Expiration date options usually expire at

4:00pm EST.

However, some options like "Index Options" expiring on 3rd Friday of the month expire in the morning at **9:30am EST.**

You will start by trading "Stock Options" instead of "Index Options".

0-DTE Options

Options that are expiring on each trading day are called 0-DTE Options.

ETFs like **SPY (S&P 500)** and **Invesco QQQ (Nasdaq-100®)** have options that are expiring every day.

0-DTE options are cheap and give **higher profit potential** but with equally **higher levels of risk.**

Pop Quiz # 2

On February 6th, 2024, following Option Expiration Dates were available on SPY (S&P 500) ETF. Complete the following.

Expiration Date	Days-To-Expiration
February 7th, 2024,	25-DTE
February 9th, 2024,	0-DTE
February 6th, 2024,	1-DTE
March 1th, 2024,	3-DTE

Strike Price

Each Option contract has an associated "Strike Price".

The "Strike Price" of an option contract does not change.

You can choose the strike price you want to trade.

The cost of each option contract depends on its "Strike Price".

EXAMPLE # 1

On Feb. 6th 2024, following were some of the SPY "Call Options" available to trade with Expiration Date March 1st, 2024.

SPY **stock price** = $493.98

Strike Price	Ask	Bid
492	$7.62	$7.30
493	$6.95	$6.67
494	$6.18	$6.08

OPTION MONEYNESS

ITM = In-The-Money

ATM = At-The-Money

OTM = Out-of-The-Money

ATM Option

The Option contract whose "Strike Price" is closest/nearest to the current stock price is called **At-The-Money Option (ATM)**

ITM Option

"**CALL Options**": Contracts whose "Strike Price" is **less** than the current stock price are called **In-The-Money Call Options.**

"**Put Options**": Contracts whose "Strike Price" is **greater** than the current stock price are called **In-The-Money Put Options.**

OTM Option

"CALL Options": Contracts whose "Strike Price" is **greater** than the current stock price are called **Out-of-The-Money Call Options.**

"Put Options": Contracts whose "Strike Price" is **less** than the current stock price are called **Out-of-The-Money Put Options.**

Pop Quiz # 3

If SPY current **stock price** is $450.
Match the following.

"Option Type"	"Strike"	"Moneyness"
Call	452	ITM
Put	449	OTM
Call	450	ITM
Call	448	ATM
Put	451	OTM

Ask & Bid Price

Ask price of an Option is the price at which you can **buy** the Option contract.

Bid price of an Option is the price at which you can **sell** the Option contract.

Ask price is always more than bid price.

Ask & Bid Spread

Ask & Bid Spread is the difference between Ask price and Bid price of the option.

Ask & Bid Spread can vary from $0.01 to $1 and sometimes even more.

On 0-DTE SPY and QQQ options, the option spread is usually $0.01.

Lot Size

All option contracts have a lot size = 100.

This means buying a single option contract with Ask Price = $1.20 will cost you 1.20x100 = $120.

RECAP

Stock price going **up** (Bullish): Buy **Calls**

Stock price going **down** (Bearish): Buy **Puts**

Options are of two types: Calls and Puts

Each Call or Put Option contract has:

"Option Type", "Expiration", "Strike Price",

"Ask Price", "Bid Price"

Making your First Trade

In your trading App like RobinHood, enter SPY in search bar. Inside SPY page, select "Trade Options". Select Expiration =**March 1st 2024**, and select option type= "**Call**". Select the option with **Strike Price = 494**. Buy one contract with **Ask Price=$6.18**. This will cost you **$618**.

Order Types

There are 3 primary order types.

Market Order

Limit Order

Stop Loss Limit Order

MARKET ORDER

Market Order: Your order gets fulfilled fastest but not at the best price.

E.g. the Ask price might be $1.20 but actual price you pay might be $1.25

You should only use this if you need to buy or sell your option immediately regardless of the price you get.

Limit Order

Limit Order: You get your desired price upon fulfillment, but it might take a while to fulfill your order.

In this order type, you provide the price (Limit Price) you want to buy the option at. Usually, your Limit Price will be $0.01 to $0.5 less than current Ask Price.

Stop Loss Limit Order

Stop Loss Limit Order: This is a Limit Order combined with a Stop Loss Limit Order.

You provide the Limit Price you want to buy the option at. At the same time, you provide a lower Stop Loss price, at which you want to sell your option in case your option loses value.

Pop Quiz # 4

(Current Date February 6th 2024)

A SPY Call Option Expiring on March 1st with Strike Price 494. If you send a Market Order, what is likely actual price?

Ask Price	Fill#1	Fill#2	Fill#3
$6.18	($6.27)	$6.10	$6.17
$7.00	$6.89	$6.99	$7.12
$2.92	$2.88	$3.02	$2.7
$0.65	$0.61	$0.68	$0.59

POP QUIZ # 5

Circle the Limit Price that is most likely
to be fulfilled fastest.

Ask Price	Limit#1	Limit#2	Limit#3
$9.20	($9.20)	$9.15	$9.18
$1.33	$1.29	$1.15	$1.31
$7.61	$7.56	$7.59	$7.45
$0.64	$0.63	$0.61	$0.45
$0.25	$0.21	$0.23	$0.18

Pricing Options

The price of an option primarily depends on

"Option Type": Call or Put

"Time to Expiration": TTE

"Strike Price": Moneyness

Option Prices also depend on other factors like market volatility or Implied Volatility. But in this book, we will only consider the above factors.

Pricing: Time to Expiration

Options with more Time to Expiration (TTE) are more expensive than options with less Time to Expiration in general.

This is because the more time an option has left before expiring, the more likely that stock price moves in its direction.

POP QUIZ # 6

(Current Date February 6th, 2024)

Below is list of option expiries and option prices (Ask). Match them in correct order. All options have same type (Call) and Strike (495) on SPY with price= $492.5

Expiration	Ask Price
February 14th, 2024,	$0.65
February 9th, 2024,	$3.85
February 6th, 2024,	$12.75
February 27th, 2024,	$7.40

Pricing: Moneyness

Options that are ITM are more expensive than options that are OTM.

"Call Options": Get **cheaper** as **Strike Price Increases**

"Put Options": Get **expensive** as **Strike Price Increases**

POP QUIZ # 7

Two SPY options both expire in 30 days. Both are "Call" options. The strike prices are 450 and 458. which strike option has lower "Ask Price"?

____

Correct Answer is: "Option with strike price = 458." This is because both are Call options on SPY with same expiration date. In such a case we know that option Ask price decreases as strike price increases.

POP QUIZ # 8

Two QQQ options both expire in 7 days. Both are "Put" options. The strike prices are 345 and 346. Which strike option has lower "Ask Price"?

____

Correct Answer is: "Option with strike price = 345." This is because both are Put options on QQQ with same expiration date. In such a case we know that option Ask price increases as strike price increases.

Pop Quiz # 9

Determine what are the option types?

Option Type   Strikes: 451 | 452| 453

___Calls___   Ask: 3.25 | 2.35| 1.50

__________   Ask: 5.00 | 4.10| 3.35

__________   Ask: 7.25 | 8.10| 9.05

__________   Ask: 1.15 | 2.35| 3.50

__________   Ask: 5.25 | 4.35| 3.10

__________   Ask: 1.25 | 0.85| 0.45

Theta Decay

Options price decreases as time goes on. This is because lesser Time TO Expiration remains. Options you bought tend to lose value as time goes on.

Options you hold overnight can lose value in the morning.

Option Delta

As stock price goes up Call options get expensive. Similarly, the Put options lose value as stock price goes up. And vice-versa.

However not all options prices move the same amount. ITM options prices move more than the OTM options.

CALL DELTA

Call Option Delta is between $0 and $1. An option with delta of $0.35 means the Call Option's price will increase by $0.35 if stock price increases by $1.

Call Options with higher strike price have lower delta than Call Options with lower Strike Prices.

Put Delta

Put Option Delta is between $0 and -$1. An option with delta of -$0.15 means the Put Option's price will decrease by $0.15 if stock price increases by $1.

Put Options with higher strike price have lower delta (close to -$1) than Puts Options with lower Strike Prices (close to $0 delta).

POP QUIZ # 10

Determine what are the option types?

Option Type

Strikes: 451 | 452| 453

_____Calls_____   Delta: 0.50 | 0.35| 0.17

_____________   Delta: -0.6 | -0.75| -0.9

_____________   Delta: -0.1 | -0.25| -0.4

_____________   Delta: 0.95 | 0.65| 0.4

_____________   Delta: 0.35 | 0.15| 0.05

_____________   Delta: -0.5 | -0.6| -0.85

Pop Quiz # 11

If the current price of SPY is $450.

A Call option on SPY with 10 DTE and strike price =455 has Ask price = $4.5. Option Delta is $0.25. If SPY price goes to $451 what will be the approximate new Ask price be.

———————

SPY price increased by $1. So, the option price will increase by $0.25 therefore new Ask price = $4.5 + $0.25 = $4.75

Pop Quiz # 12

If the current price of QQQ is $350.

A Put option on QQQ with 30 DTE and strike price =348 has Ask price = $5.7. Option Delta is -$0.45. If QQQ price goes to $351 what will be the approximate new Ask price be.

____

QQQ price increased by $1. So, the option price will change by delta of -$0.45 therefore new Ask price = $5.7 - $0.45 = $5.25

Delta & Moneyness

$0.5 Delta Call Option is ATM.

Calls with delta more than $0.5 are ITM.

Calls with delta less than $0.5 are OTM.

-$0.5 Delta Put Option is ATM.

Puts with delta between -$0.5 & -$1 are ITM.

Call Options with delta between -$0.5 & $0 are OTM.

Pop Quiz # 13

Choose correct moneyness?

Type	Delta		Moneyness
Call	0.65		(ITM) | ATM | OTM
Call	0.50		ITM | ATM | OTM
Put	-0.95		ITM | ATM | OTM
Put	-0.35		ITM | ATM | OTM
Call	0.25		ITM | ATM | OTM
Put	-0.50		ITM | ATM | OTM

OPTION CHARM

As time goes on the delta of all options also changes. This is called Charm.

ITM options become more sensitive to stock price changes (hence delta get closer to $1 or -$1).

OTM options become less sensitive to stock price changes (hence delta get closer to $0)

Calls Charm

Let's say you bought a SPY 0-DTE Call option with delta of $0.40 at 9:45am on day of expiration. 2 hours go by and now the option delta is $0.25.

If SPY price goes up by $1 now, the call option price will increase by $0.25 instead of $0.40.

PUTS CHARM

Let's say you bought a QQQ 0-DTE Put option with delta of -$0.60 at 10:00am on day of expiration. 2 hours go by and now the option delta is -$0.90.

If QQQ price goes down by $1 now, the put option price will increase by $0.90 instead of $0.60.

Charm Example

Let's say you bought a SPY 0-DTE Call option with delta of $0.60 at 9:45am for Ask price of **$1.50**. Immediately SPY drops by $1. This causes Call's delta to reduce to $0.3 and the new Ask is $1.05.

Now SPY stays at this level for 2 hours, the option delta becomes $0.1 due to Charm and Ask =$1 due to Theta. If SPY finally bounces back up $1, since option delta is $0.1 now, the option price is roughly $1 + $0.1 = **$1.10**. Although SPY price came back to its original price level, the option lost $1.10-$1.50 = -$0.40 due to Theta and Charm.

Options Gamma

The Gamma of an Option is the change in its Delta if the stock price increases by $1

E.g. if a SPY Call option has delta of $0.6 and SPY moves up by $1 resulting in new delta of $0.8 then:

Option Gamma = $0.8-$0.6 = $0.2

Intrinsic Option Value

"Call": If the stock price is below option's Strike Price, then intrinsic value =0.

If stock price is above Strike Price, then Intrinsic value of Call option is "Stock Price" minus "Strike Price".

"Put": If the stock price is above option's Strike Price, then intrinsic value =0.

If stock price is below Strike Price, then Intrinsic value of Put option is "Strike Price" minus "Stock Price".

Simply Stated

"ATM or OTM Call": Intrinsic value =0.

"ITM Call": Intrinsic value = "Stock Price" minus "Strike Price".

"ATM or OTM Put": Intrinsic value =0.

"ITM Put": Intrinsic value = "Strike Price" minus "Stock Price".

Pop Quiz # 14

Calculate the Intrinsic Value of following

Type	Strike	Stock Price	Intrinsic Value
Call	450	455	$5.00
Call	320	321	$
Put	450	448	$
Put	11	9	$
Call	120	119.5	$
Put	450	455	$

Extrinsic Option Value

Extrinsic Value = "Ask Price" minus "Intrinsic Value"

The extrinsic value of an option reduces to zero due to Option Theta as time passes.

Roughly, if an option has 100 DTE, then over the next day, the Option will lose around 1% of its extrinsic value.

Extrinsic Value →→Theta→→ $0

POP QUIZ # 15

If a OTM 0-DTE Call Option has Ask price of $0.80 at 12pm EST. I.e. there are 4 hours remaining before option expiry

Over the next 1 hour roughly what % of option value will decay due to Theta?

____

The correct answer is 25%. This is because option is OTM so Ask = Extrinsic Value. It has to decay to 0 in next 4 hours, so 1/4th or 25% decays in the next hour.

RISKS IN OPTIONS TRADING

Options are considered one of the riskiest products to trade.

You Call or Put option can lose all its value within a few minutes or matter of a day.

Careful allocation of small budgets to each trade is the first line of defense.

Risk Factors

Overly large trade sizes

Improper use of Order Types

Movement in stock price (Delta)

Sudden Large stock price movement (Gamma)

Time decay of option value (Theta)

Waiting too long for recovery (Charm)

Human Error (Your mistakes)

Lot Size Confusion

All option contracts have a lot size of 100.

A common mistake is to not consider 100x factor when sizing the trade.

A single option contract with Ask = $3.50 will cost you $350.

So the capital at risk is 100 times more.

Pop Quiz # 16

For each of following trades compute the total cost incurred (premium paid).

Ask	# of Contracts	Premium Paid
4.45	1	$445
4.45	10	$
0.65	100	$
8.65	5	$
1.25	1000	$

Tax Consideration

Most of your profits from your options will be taxed at Short Term Capital Gains Rate.

Index Options under section 1256 provide a 60/40 Long Term & Short-Term Rate tax treatment.

Consult a tax professional for details.

POP QUIZ # 17

You purchased 20 contracts of a Call option for Aks Price= 7.00. Three days later you sold the 20 contracts for a Bid price =12.00.

At Short Term Capital Gain Tax Rate of 20%, what is your expected Tax Bill?

Your total cost (premium paid) was = 7.00x100 x 20 = $14000. You sold the options for total price =12.00x100x20 = $2400. Your profit is =$24000-$14000 = $10,000. At 20% Tax Rate, your Tax Owed = 20% of $10,000 = $2000

PAPER TRADE PRACTICE # 1

On Feb 6th, 2024, you buy 1 contract of Tesla's (TSLA) Call option. Option Expires on March 15th, 2024, with a strike price of $190. At the time TSLA price =$186.5. The Ask price is $9.2

What is total cost of the trade? What is the most you can lose on this trade?

__________, __________

Your total cost is = 9.2x100x1 = $920. We multiply by 100 here because all options have a lot size of 100. You can lose your entire investment of $920.

PAPER TRADE PRACTICE # 2

If a OTM 10-DTE Call Option has Ask price of $15. Over the next 1 day roughly what % of option value will decay due to Theta?

____

The correct answer is 10%. This is because the option is OTM so Ask Price = Extrinsic Value. Extrinsic Value has to decay to 0 in the next 10 days, so $1/10^{th}$ or 10% decays in the next 1 day.

Paper Trade Practice # 3

On March 3rd, 2024, you buy 1 contract of Amazon's (AMZN) Put option. The option expires on May 17th, 2024, with a strike price of $95. At the time, AMZN's price is $100. The Ask price is $7.3.

What is the total cost of the trade? What is the most you can lose on this trade?

______________, ______________

Your total cost is = 7.3x100x1 = $730. You can lose your entire investment of $730.

PAPER TRADE PRACTICE # 4

On April 5th, 2024, you buy 2 contracts of Netflix's (NFLX) Call option. The option expires on June 10th, 2024, with a strike price of $450. At the time, NFLX's price is $440. The Ask price is $21.5.

What is the total cost of the trade? What is the most you can lose on this trade?

______________ , ______________

Your total cost is = 21.5x100x2 = $4,300. You can lose your entire investment of $4,300.

Paper Trade Practice # 5

You own 1 contract of Apple's (AAPL) Call option with a delta of 0.25. The current stock price is $145. If AAPL's stock price increases by $1, approximately how much the price of your option change?

Option Price Change: _______________

The option's price will roughly increase by $0.25 for every $1 increase in the stock price, meaning the option's price will increase by $0.25.

Paper Trade Practice # 6

An out-of-the-money (OTM) Put option on Amazon (AMZN) with a 20-DTE has an Ask price of $25. Over the next 1 day, what is the approximate percentage decay of the option's value due to Theta?

Estimated Theta Decay: __________

The correct answer is 5%. This is because the option is OTM so Ask Price = Extrinsic Value. Extrinsic Value has to decay to 0 in the next 20 days, so 1/20th or 5% decays in the next 1 day.

Paper Trade Practice # 7

Calculate the Intrinsic Value of the following

Type	Strike	Stock Price	Intrinsic Value
Call	100	103	$
Call	525	530	$
Put	20	25	$
Put	123	118	$
Call	760	800	$
Put	430	428.5	$

PAPER TRADE PRACTICE # 8

On July 4th, 2024, you buy 5 contracts of Intel's (INTC) Put option. The option expires on September 19th, 2024, with a strike price of $48. At the time, INTC's price is $50. The Ask price is $12.8.

What is the total cost of the trade? What is the most you can lose on this trade?

___________, ___________

Your total cost is = 12.8x100x5 = $6400. You can lose your entire investment of $6400.

Paper Trade Practice # 9

What is the Intrinsic value of a Call option with Delta $0.30.

____

If the Ask Price of the same option is $2.10. Then what is its Extrinsic Value

____

The Intrinsic Value is 0, since the option is OTM (Delta is above $0.5). Since the Intrinsic Value is $0, the Extrinsic Value equals its Ask Price.

Paper Trade Practice # 10

On September 10th, 2024, you buy 1 contract of Disney's (DIS) Put option. The option expires on November 21st, 2024, with a strike price of $125. At the time, DIS's price is $130. The Ask price is $6.7.

What is the total cost of the trade? What is the most you can lose on this trade?

___________, ___________

Your total cost is = 6.7X100X1 = $670. You can lose your entire investment of $670.

You bought a SPY 0-DTE Call Option with Delta=$0.40 at 10am. SPY stock price did not change for the next 2 hours. At 12pm, the Delta of your option is now $0.25. What is responsible for the decrease in option delta?

Gamma | Theta | Charm | Vega

Correct Answer is Charm.

PAPER TRADE PRACTICE # 12

You purchased 10 contracts of a Call option for Aks Price= 5.00. Three days later you sold the 10 contracts for a Bid price =9.00.

At Short Term Capital Gain Tax Rate of 20%, what is your expected Tax Bill?

Your total cost (premium paid) was = 5.00x100 x 10 = $5000. You sold the options for total price =9.00x100x10 = $9000. Your profit is =$9000-$5000 = $4,000. At 20% Tax Rate, your Tax Owed = 20% of $4,000 = $800

PAPER TRADE PRACTICE # 13

On November 15th, 2024, you buy 1 contract of Pfizer's (PFE) Put option. The option expires on January 16th, 2025, with a strike price of $38. At the time, PFE's price is $40. The Ask price is $1.9.

What is the total cost of the trade? What is the most you can lose on this trade?

________________ , ______________

Your total cost is = 1.9x100x1 = $190. You can lose your entire investment of $190.

Paper Trade Practice # 14

You are considering buying a Put option on Boeing (BA) with a delta of -0.35. The current stock price is $220. Based on the delta, is this option likely to be ITM or OTM?

Delta: -0.35

Option Status: _____________

A delta of -0.35 suggests the option is likely out-of-the-money (OTM), as put options with deltas closer to 0 are more likely to be OTM.

About the Author

Dr. Adan Abbasi is a dentist and an author based out of Boston. Beyond her professional interests in dentistry, she is passionate about children's education and advocating financial literacy.

This book is the result of her experiences in learning and practicing stocks and options investing.

www.ingramcontent.com/pod-product-compliance
Lightning Source LLC
Chambersburg PA
CBHW081952160726
47999CB00008B/2598